A Walk into Nature

A BOOK BY
ZIA UR REHMAN

BLUEROSE PUBLISHERS
India | U.K.

Copyright © Zia ur Rehman 2024

All rights reserved by author. No part of this publication may be reproduced, stored in a retrieval system or transmitted in any form or by any means, electronic, mechanical, photocopying, recording or otherwise, without the prior permission of the author. Although every precaution has been taken to verify the accuracy of the information contained herein, the publisher assumes no responsibility for any errors or omissions. No liability is assumed for damages that may result from the use of information contained within.

BlueRose Publishers takes no responsibility for any damages, losses, or liabilities that may arise from the use or misuse of the information, products, or services provided in this publication.

For permissions requests or inquiries regarding this publication, please contact:

BLUEROSE PUBLISHERS
www.BlueRoseONE.com
info@bluerosepublishers.com
+91 8882 898 898
+4407342408967

ISBN: 978-93-6783-021-5

Cover design: Shivam
Typesetting: Namrata Saini

First Edition: December 2024

This book is dedicated to my beloved father who guided me in every walk of life, and to my daughter who constantly inspired me to write poems about Nature.

Contents

	Foreword	vii
1.	An Evening on the Sea-shore	1
2.	Wonders of Nature	3
3.	Kashmir	4
4.	The Killers' Fury	5
5.	The Loss of a Magnificent Tree	6
6.	The Deep Melancholy	7
7.	In Remembrance of Someone	9
8.	The Road to the Scenic Mountains	10
9.	True Happiness	11
10.	Do Not Fear The Passage Of Time	12
11.	A Lovely Child	13
12.	Tranquillity in Nature	14
13.	The Beautiful Moon	15
14.	Nature is a Great Teacher	16
15.	Rain on the Beach	17
16.	A Walk into Nature	18
17.	The Morning Light	19
18.	The Eternal Mountains	20
19.	Shadow of the Forest	21
20.	An Old Scholar	22
21.	A Cheerful House	23

22. Keep moving in the stream of life 24
23. Mist in the Mountains 25
24. Healing Shades 26
25. A Scary Adventure 27
    Acknowledgements 30

Foreword

Nature is full of wonders. Whenever I visited a hill-station, I was fascinated by the beauty of mountains, rivers and lakes and their memories remained fresh in my mind. I was also shocked to see the ongoing deforestation and the loss of greenery on the mountains. I realized that such beautiful landscapes must be cherished and preserved and for this reason, I indulged myself with writing poems on the beautiful theme of Nature.

I hope that my poems will serve the purpose of creating awareness and my dear readers will like them and derive pleasure from them.

Zia ur Rehman

November 18, 2024

An Evening on the Sea-shore

How beautiful it is to stand on the peaceful shore
And watch the sun going down the horizon!
The sparkling waters of the sea
Change their colours to orange shades.
The twittering birds that gather at shores
Have already departed to their abodes.

And I the solo traveller
Gaze at the far end of the sea.
Where my thoughts take a new shape
And make me happy in this colourful evening,
Where I can praise God for
His wonderful creation with a contented soul.

I move my steps on the sands of shore
Where I meet a lovely child
Selling some balloons for his daily bread,
His shadow falls on the glimmering sand;
And towards me he extends his tiny arms
Imploring for some cash in hand.

He wishes to sell his multi-coloured balloons
For a scanty price in the ending day.
How nice a feeling comes upon me
When I buy his balloons with love!
And his face turns into a smiling one
With a shining radiance on his lips.

He looks towards the setting sun,
And thanks God for His mercy on him.
I move forward carrying the bunch of balloons
To walk beyond the beach till dusk.
My feelings and emotions have a new charm now,
And a surge of happiness more deeply goes rushing into my heart.

Wonders of Nature

When you sit in the lap of Nature
You find your heart beat with pleasure,
The silence of trees and the smile of flowers
Take you into the depth of leisure.

The sun rays fall upon the gardens,
And the rivers sparkle with delight;
The daytime offers great blessings
And the nights are full of spiritual light.

The myriad wonders of Nature engulf the countryside,
The brooks flow like a music soft and soothing;
They take with them the petals of flowers,
And the lovers pick them up with smile so charming.

The birds take shelter among the branches of trees,
When the night shows the first sign of arrival;
And fly away in the morning light,
To take part in the struggle for survival.

Oh! What a bliss it is to watch
The beautiful landscape of mountains so high;
The glory of serenity and beautiful sunlight
Falls upon the meadows where lovers do not say goodbye.

What can be better than the deep recollections of vivid memories
Aided by the touch of tranquillity?
Contentment and happiness are felt so deeply
Rich with the splendour of Nature's creativity.

Kashmir

Oh yes! I love this amazing place on earth,
So lush green and wonderful;
It is the paradise on earth,
It is Kashmir—its unmatched splendour is delightful.

Its landscape is so stunning,
Its purity shines on the loving faces of children;
All around me I find them exhilarated,
Their smiles are full of innocent fun.

I had a deep desire to imagine that
I would see its lofty mountains with snow-capped peaks;
And now I am present here in this lovely scenery of Kashmir,
Mesmerized by the delicious sunshine falling on my cheeks.

I'm in a fantastic world now,
Feeling exuberant in Nature's glory;
Every season is spectacular here,
How can I ever forget this place of picturesque beauty!

Dal Lake is so magnificent in its charm,
Mountains here form a great reflection;
It is the heaven on earth – the majestic Kashmir,
Its incredible beauty is beyond all words of expression.

The Killers' Fury

A leaf whispers to another leaf,
"Be alert,
Turn around,
There is a man with an axe,
He looks very dangerous;
His eyes are blood-shot,
His desires are impure,
His intentions are evil,
We must be careful."

The other leaf turns around and gets terrified,
It starts rustling and looks above for a dense foliage;
The whole tree trembles,
The birds fly away and leave the tree alone;
They make eerie sounds and tell the tree to beware of other men,
Who seem to be ferocious with weapons in their hands.

Suddenly a strange horrific sound travels the air,
And there is a thud of explosion;
A branch falls down
With a canopy,
And soon the others separate from their roots,
Writhing with pain helplessly under the destruction by evil-doers,
The killers who have decided to devastate
The life of their family.

The Loss of a Magnificent Tree

The big, stately tree has fallen down,
Cut down by sharp axes with a tremor of shock
To make a way for a block of flats,
And to widen the road for an easy walk.

Hardly there was any consideration of loss
By the ordering authorities
Who took the tree as an obstacle on the road,
And permitted its killing to avoid complexities.

Birds fled away with fear,
And left their nests in the ancient tree
Which was about to fall down
By the continuous brutal strokes to disengage it free.

It wasn't an easy task to kill a mighty tree,
Thick ropes and sharp knives were brought about,
To uproot it with great force,
So quickly ordered by the men of political clout.

For a tree of such beauty and magnificence,
'Killing' is a better word than 'cutting',
The authorities plan to make modern flats in place of old trees,
And to develop the roads for fast urbanizing.

Nature has once again lost its majestic pearl
Which used to give shade to tired travellers,
How many more big and small trees,
Will be lost forever for giving space to artificial city developers?

The Deep Melancholy

Some sounds are so crushing that they are never heard,
But they are full of vibrations and affect the society to the core;
The sound of pain, the sound of torture, the sound of torment, the sound of fury, the sound of teasing, the sound of molestation;
These brutal sounds which are so hard to endure.

Corruption in the mind is the deadliest one,
Which leads to the fatal diseases for mankind;
The message of true love has been reduced to mere preaching,
All the reforms look like mirages of a strange kind.

Where is the true love gone and lost?
The love which bound the two persons together;
The love which eased the movement of thoughts
And spread the healthy flow of air far and near.

The love which had far-reaching dimensions,
That made the whole landscape of families so strong;
The love which did not have pre-conceived notions
To prove each other right and wrong.

Machines have taken the toll on human heart,
They have taken us away from Nature and humanity;
They have replaced empathy with false sympathy,
And our emotions are lost in the desert of technology.

But still there is hope in the arms of Nature,
Our deep melancholy may turn into joy and happiness;
The spite and gloomy state of mind,
Will be replaced by the glow of everlasting cheerfulness.

In Remembrance of Someone

I waited for you eagerly
To join me as a traveller,
A solo journey I was embarking on
To see the beautiful Nature with joy and wonder.

You had your own reasons for not joining me
In this thrilling adventure,
But if you had come with me,
It would turn out to be a lifetime venture.

Travel teaches toleration and patience
And Nature has a healing touch,
The beautiful mountains and valleys
Broaden our minds so much.

How can I ever forget
The mesmerizing landscapes I have seen,
It changed my perception altogether
Being in the Valley of Kashmir so green.

I greatly miss you in my journey
I feel like a solo wanderer,
And every beautiful aspect of Nature
Tells me a difference between traveller and non-traveller.

The Road to the Scenic Mountains

Take your silent way through the hills,
Move forward like the flowing stream;
You may face some difficult terrain
But keep on walking to fulfil your dream.

The road is rough, the journey is long,
Be a walking wanderer with the spirit of a song;
The breeze is cool on the higher altitude,
Embrace it with open arms as you move along.

You may find some rocks with sharp edges and slopes,
But they are the stepping stones on the height of adventure;
And soon you'll find the beautiful valleys
And the brooks and fountains with their murmuring and pleasure.

Each bend on the roads will surprise you with a new vista
Of the beautiful mountains and the skies of magnificent colours;
The boughs of trees welcome you on the way
And embrace you like the graceful arms of lovers.

True Happiness

Where is true happiness in the world?
This was the question I asked my father;
Father said, "Dear son, Look inside your heart,
It will answer your query very well."
I couldn't understand what he said,
But I remained quiet and sought the answer in my heart to whisperingly tell.
The next day again I asked my father where the true happiness is,
Then he put for me a question so interesting.

'Are you contented and satisfied?' he said.
'Yes, of course, Daddy! was my response.
Father said, "My dear son, Contentment is happiness,
True happiness is inside you.
When you're contented, you're at peace,
And you have got the answer to your question with ease."

Do Not Fear The Passage Of Time

Time passes quickly and seems to be in a hurry,
Too short to enjoy anything;
Sadness and Darkness creep into us,
And move in profound silence taking hold of everything.

Both want to remove from existence Happiness and Light,
And create the atmosphere of horror and fear;
Unaware of the power of Soul
Which can surely overcome the fear haunting so near.

To feel the stillness of Time,
We have to make our souls pure and powerful;
Patience, kindness and love for goodness
Will take us on the path of God the most merciful.

Happiness and Light cannot be terrified by anything,
If the souls are beautiful, strong and awake;
Time only troubles those who remain away from Nature,
Who take pleasure in doing wrong and do not realize
their mistake.

A Lovely Child

You are a dear, lovely child
With a beautiful, cheerful smile;
You run about here and there
Amusing us by your funny style.

Your eyes are green and very fair,
And curly mould of lovely hair
That scatter round your head in shine;
You nod it and make us laugh so sincere.

Your loving grandfather kept you in his arms
When you were a little baby;
He caressed your soft cheeks so gently
And you smiled at him and cried and laughed with full intensity.

You are a fond reflection of your wonderful parents
Who take care of you in your every need;
They weep for you when you fall down sometimes
Playing in your childish pranks paying no heed.

You imitate very nicely with stooping shoulders
Your pretty grandmother when she walks in the room;
Dear child, you're a wonderful boy
An inspiration and a hope for anyone in gloom.

Tranquillity in Nature

How can our minds remain in patience and peace
When our busy schedules are no longer at ease?
We keep on rushing in the race of urban life,
And then we criticize Time for causing disaster and disease.

Time is not so fast in the serenity of Nature,
It sometimes stops also in the calm mountains and rills;
In the murmuring brooks flowing past the trees,
And the blossoms shaking in the breeze with thrills.

Nature's always at work,
Whether in night or by day;
Cheerful days and lovely nights
Make us wise in their own way.

There's melody in the sounds of songbirds,
We can learn from them how to relax in tranquillity;
Nightingales fill the days and nights with beautiful tunes,
They have their own soft music when we listen to them in silence and nobility.

The Beautiful Moon

I take a walk outside on a clear night,
The weather is cool and the air is crisp;
I can see the stars shining and the moon smiling,
Touching softly its silver rays on my cheek and the lip.

The leaves are shaking in the wind so nicely,
And I walk and sing praise to the God Almighty
Who has designed the moon with such beauty and glory,
Reflection of the pure whiteness of light in elegant nicety.

The moon is the cause for the tides to rise,
And to maintain the life's equilibrium in full;
The inspiration for some people to become the painters
And motivation for the lovers to always stay hopeful.

Every shape of moon has its own beauty and charm,
Whether it be crescent or the full moon in bloom;
I walk through the valleys and mountains
And the moon always guides me in situations of gloom.

Nature is a Great Teacher

The weather is so cool and calm,
Why not enjoy and take up a ride on the hills?
Forgetting the worries and troubles of the day,
Let us derive pleasure in the beautiful rills.

Nature fills the world with breathtaking wonders,
It has a great message in the flowing streams and rivers;
There are lessons for us in the flight of birds flocking together,
In the symmetrical designs of amazing webs of spiders.

The majestic sea teaches us
A great lesson of enormity and contentment;
The rising and falling waves
Encourage us to face the resentment.

The flowers exhale fragrance and the moments rapidly pass,
The bees move from one flower to the other humming a nice song;
The grasshopper leaps up on the sun-kissed grass,
Nature motivates us beautifully on life's difficult roads which appear so long.

Rain on the Beach

The sea brings back fond memories
Of childhood days with charming splendour;
When pleasant thoughts captivate me,
I indulge myself in nostalgic wonder.

The moon and stars were all so bright,
The night was full of calm and peace;
And I sat cool on the shore of sea
To look at the glimmer of waves with ease.

Perfect stillness was in the air,
The stars were shining like lamps on the sea;
The sea tides were lapping the shore so gently
Like a musical song of a lover in glee.

A sudden change the weather felt now,
The whispers of breeze grew more aloud;
The waves of sea began to roar
And the wind filled the sky with a big cloud.

Soon the raindrops were felt on my skin,
And I stood up and moved on the edge of sea;
The drizzling rain glistened down my hair
And the sheer passion of ecstasy was aroused in me.

Then a sudden rush of air
Touched with raindrops my hands and cheeks;
And I gazed upon the sea so vast
With my dreams revived for sweet melodies.

A Walk into Nature

The sight of mountains aroused in me
Thoughts of longing from the window of my room;
I quickly collected myself for a beautiful walk
In the Nature to see the flowers in bloom.

I am a curious traveller,
I prefer to walk on a solitary lane;
The babbling of a brook in the valley
Creates in me a reverie like a musical rain.

The children greet me on the way,
My heart overflows with the joy of ecstasy;
The melody of birds in the trees
Soothes my nerves for a strange discovery.

A Walk into Nature is the most promising
When the sky is overcast and the breeze is quiet;
Blessed are those who admire the beauty of clouds
With eager eyes brimming with delight.

The Morning Light

O the beautiful morning!
Your light is so inspiring;
It has captivated my thoughts and feelings
By your glory so enchanting.

The sun rises in its beauty and calm,
Its wonderful rays falling on my half-bare arm;
The sky is filled with the joys of heaven,
The chirping of birds is a sweet alarm.

The leaves are shaking in their wakeful appearance,
Possessing in them the undiscovered mysteries;
The earth has shed off its nightly teasing,
The cuckoos and doves sing the glory of trees.

The morning light is so magnificent and splendid,
It has the spiritual beauty of awakening;
What a picture of colours is all around!
A new day is born with the sunbeams streaming.

The Eternal Mountains

Nice is the distant view of eternal mountains,
Blue colours turning into white in the shining rain;
Heaped upon each other are those beautiful rolling hills,
A look at them makes me happy and takes away my pain.

The enchanting beauty of the wooded hills,
Is enough to gladden my heart;
I forget the worries and cares of the day,
From these lush green mountains I do not wish to depart.

The rising sun above the silent trees
Makes the landscape picturesque on mountain peaks;
It is a great and wonderful scene,
Enough to refresh and enliven the routine for weeks.

Shadow of the Forest

Every bend of the mountain road opens into new vistas,
The beautiful trees give us fresh air for breathing;
There is no pain of noisy disturbance,
The faces of innocent children with sunshine are beaming.

Lying down in the shadow of the forest is a cool mystery,
The breeze whispers a beautiful song;
We are what our thoughts make us,
Let us enjoy Nature as we move along.

Let us fall asleep in the peace of valley,
Let the shadow of the forest rest upon us;
The sweet murmur of the flowing brook
Will erase the effects of what a trouble does.

Let us touch gently the blades of grass,
They are so bright and green in this colourful vale;
Don't be hasty in this awesome weather,
Enjoy every moment without any fear to fall down or fail.

Nature is full of miracles and wonders,
Its blessings never cease to exist even in stormy thunders.

An Old Scholar

I found an old man sitting on the rocky shore,
Holding a book in his hand, his spectacles on nose;
Near to him was a vast tumultuous sea and an uproar
Of waves tossing as a comment on the transitory shows.

He seemed to be lonely in this big world of fame,
A world full of people but not friendly to someone
Who wanted to give his best and survive through his name,
Now sadness occupied his thoughts and he talked to none.

There were some whispers on the beach among the visitors,
That this old man had been a great scholar;
But due to unbearable circumstances faced by him,
The man looked very despondent and poor.

The old man got up and closed his book,
Ruminating about his past life against the less changing sea;
A flock of birds flew over his head encouraging him to look
At the puffy clouds drifting away like a shapeless tree.

A Cheerful House

A cheerful house is a wonderful house,
It is not noisy but a peaceful house;
Where love and affection is a noble theme,
And no one dares to shout and scream.

Where true knowledge is the goal of life,
And no place is given to strife;
Where children are given an education of care,
And adults practise a gentle behaviour.

Where visions are built for a healthy nation,
And goals are set to remove all corruption;
Where the books are read and understood with pride,
And imagination is enhanced far and wide.

Such a house is always a happy house,
Which never ever becomes a gloomy house.

Keep moving in the stream of life

Life moves on like a flowing stream,
Feel happy in its flow and enjoy each moment;
Do not frown at the swift movement of Time,
Set your own pace of life steady and constant.

When the lonely children in the dark nights feel sad and scared,
They rush to their mothers' laps to rest and snuggle;
The business of daily life moves on and on,
With the profit and loss of everyday's struggle.

Do not keep yourself in sad thoughts
For the diminishing physical beauty with the Time's quick run;
Take pride in Nature's everlasting treasures,
Where every hour is sweeter than the previous one.

Keep moving in the stream of life,
Moss is not gathered on the rolling stones.

Mist in the Mountains

It is a wonderful sight,
The mist taking hold of the houses within no time;
Entering the mountains of Mussoorie so gently,
Enveloping the trees and the roads in a beauty so sublime.

It is an exhilarating scene,
Enough to push me in the realm of dreams;
The elegance of Nature and its enriched landscape,
Fills me with freshness of thoughts like exotic streams.

How quickly the weather changes here,
The clarity of winding roads becomes obscure;
The lofty hills get engulfed by curling mist,
And I stop myself to enjoy its magical pace so sudden and pure.

Mussoorie is truly called the Queen of Hills,
It has its own majestic charm and splendour;
The beautiful landscape with a great natural beauty,
Is a blessing and boon and a joy forever.

Healing Shades

Make your journey into the splendid scenery
Which reigns in the forest so wide and dense;
The forest that is full of shades of trees,
The rustle of leaves, the chirp of birds and a lot of wisdom and sense.

Listen to the melody of nightingales and cuckoo birds,
They sweeten the air with divine musical charm;
The majestic pace of tigers and the running of deer
Are a wonderful sight for Nature lovers who do not cause any harm.

There is comfort in the healing shades of trees,
The winds meet them and make them swing;
Time is slow in the natural world of forest,
Embrace each season, be it Autumn or the Spring.

A Scary Adventure

Six sturdy boys went up the hill,
Being zealous and full of lovely plans;
To make the most of their adventurous trip,
They had left their homes early for some big chance.

They had smile on their lips,
For it was a thrilling adventure;
They wished to explore the mountains,
And feel the fresh breezy air.

As they walked a lonely road,
They felt whispers of tall trees;
The morning air was cool and calm,
But the boys sat down on their knees.

Suddenly the weather began to change,
And the clouds could be seen floating on the hills;
The breeze turned into the howling wind,
It was an unexpected test for the boys' trekking skills.

The morning light transformed into darkness,
The boys struggled to climb the hilly road;
A force of wind kept pulling them down,
They found it difficult to balance their load.

A sudden drizzle fell on their faces,
They wanted to take some shelter ahead;
The rain was quick to become heavy,
And the boys were caught in the shower of dread.

The rain hid the range of hills,
And the bends on roads became invisible;
The boys could see no hills now,
And their journey turned fearful and miserable.

One of the boys caught a glimpse of a shed,
Located somewhere down the bending road;
The boys picked up their bags at once,
To move for safety and their faces glowed.

The wind howled and changed to stormy weather,
The shed looked somewhat horrible and scary;
The boys who had planned their adventure so well,
Were caught between hope and fear not at all imaginary.

The fear was real and the life was precious,
But the boys had no option except to move downhill;
They trudged towards the shed and reached there by the winding road,
The shed was desolate and the boys uttered a cry so shrill.

The biggest of the boys tried to open the door of shed,
It creaked and made a terrible sound;
It was wobbly but locked from inside,
And the boys felt themselves to be bound.

The howling wind made them faint and frightful,
They were unable to proceed any further;
But the respite came in the form of an old man
Who was seen approaching them in this terrible weather.

The old man gasped and stopped near the boys,
And warned them not to open the door of shed;
He narrated some strange stories about it,
And told them it was a haunted shed.

He guided them towards the direction of a village
Which was on the other side of a huge mountain;
The boys picked up their luggage so fast,
And thanked the old man who vanished like a fountain.

The rain stopped and the wind changed to a pleasant breeze,
The mist disappeared and the hills became clear;
All the six boys sped up towards the village,
And pursued their scary adventure with much less fear.

Acknowledgements

I would like to express my sincere gratitude to my parents, especially my father who inspired in me the love of reading books of great writers. My mother kept on motivating me to write verses.

I am obliged to my wife and my daughter who encouraged me and provided me unconditional support in the process of writing.

I am thankful to my publishers whose optimism and faith in me inspired me to complete this book of poetry.

www.ingramcontent.com/pod-product-compliance
Lightning Source LLC
LaVergne TN
LVHW061623070526
838199LV00078B/7398